MW01153854

KAYDEN IS DIFFERENT!

by Roosevelt Mitchell III, M. Ed
Illustrations by Chris House

This book is dedicated to my
son and daughter, Kayden and Kameelah.
Every day I wake up and I try to be a better man
and somebody that both of you can be proud
of. No matter how many books that I write, my
greatest creation will always be you.
Daddy loves you.

Hi, my name is Kayden!
I am five years old.
I don't know what happened, but
I was born different from other kids.

My parents tell me that I am just like my brother James, but I don't look like him or the other kids on television or in my neighborhood.

My right arm is shorter than the left and I was born with only seven fingers.

When I go places with my mommy, everyone looks at me funny.

Even grown people stare at me!

I don't like it because it makes me feel strange.

Most of the kids in my neighborhood are scared of me and ask questions like "How did your hand get like that?" or "Does it hurt to only have two fingers?"

This makes me feel very sad because I just want to play with them.

I only have one friend to play with and she does not care that I look different.
She is not scared of my arm and doesn't ask me mean questions.

Her name is Ashley and she lives next door!

I visit Ashley's house all the time.

We play many games together, like racing, hide-go-seek and tag.

I feel good when I am with Ashley!

If only all the other kids in my neighborhood were nice like her and were not scared of me.

I would love having more friends.

I'd show them how good I am at other games such as basketball, kickball and checkers.

Then we could all play together!

CPSIA information can be obtained
at www.ICGtesting.com
Printed in the USA
LVIC04n0735290116
472811LV00002B/2